God Chose To Save

D1113570

God Chose To Save

**Why Man *Cannot* And *Will Not*
Be Saved Apart From Election**

by

Joseph M. Bianchi

Joint publication with

EVANGELICAL PRESS, Faverdale North Industrial Estate, Darlington, DL3 0PH, England.
(Evangelical Press USA P. O. Box 825, Webster, MA 14580, USA).
e-mail: sales@evangelicalpress.org
www.evangelicalpress.org

and

CALVARY PRESS, Box 805, Amityville, NY 11701, USA.
www.calvarypress.com

First published 2001
Second printing 2004

British Library Cataloguing in Publication Data available.

ISBN 0 85234 497 X

Printed in United Sates of America

Dedication

This book is dedicated to all those who truly seek the heart
and will of God and to my lovely wife Monica, and daughter
Christina, who have endured through the various stages of
my sanctification.

Contents

Introduction

There is perhaps no subject more discussed, more argued and more vilified than the concept of the sovereignty of God in salvation. Yet, there is simply no way to navigate around this most important subject. This present work does not pretend to be the last word on the issue. Indeed, many a tome has been written on the concept of God's sovereignty in the life of a Christian. However, what will be insisted here is that there is always room for looking at the issue from another angle, and this is where we take our departure.

One of the major problems engendered from both sides of the issue, that is, from those championing 'free will' as opposed to those who insist on absolute election, is the problem of 'proof texting'. This problem is akin to a boxing match: Each boxer tries to land as many punches as possible in the hopes that his opponent will simply fall over. Thus, verses are stacked together like so many building blocks upon the opposing argument until, it is hoped, all collapses into a useless heap.

This book will attempt to do something different. Specifically, we will attempt to look at the particular themes that speak to the issue. We will keep in mind that God's word speaks to us in themes, not just specific texts, and we will see in all of this God's overall plan, rather than a dizzying array of verses.

While much argumentation on this subject has been fuelled by emotion, it is hoped that this straightforward analysis will yield a clear and useable product. It is to that end that we approach this subject. More importantly, our ultimate goal is to bring glory to the Lord Jesus Christ who can save to the uttermost!

1.
The Problem

Over the years behaviorist psychology has tried to implant in our minds the idea that man is basically good; that he has good intentions, innately wants to help others; and when faced with a choice with doing 'the good' or doing evil, chances are his instincts will be to choose good.

But the Bible, God's inerrant Word, says something quite different about man: he is born a sinner with a proclivity toward evil thoughts and actions. He is, to use a vernacular term, 'damaged goods' in need of redemption. But what are the circumstances of this redemption? Does God, in His Sovereign will save, or is there a synergism; a working together of God and Man? This question strikes at the heart of the issue. It also begs another question: Who is ultimately in control of a person's salvation?

Stated more specifically, this question comes out as: 'What, indeed, is the gospel?'

You may immediately reply, 'Man is lost in sin and cannot save himself. Jesus died in the place of sinners. If we receive him as our Saviour, we become 'born again' and escape condemnation.'

True enough, but how is this salvation applied? Do we make a 'decision' for Jesus? That is to say, do we weigh the evidence, ponder a bit, and of our own free will ask Jesus into our life? If this is the case, then man is in control of his salvation. You may immediately reply, 'But God draws us to him!'

Now we are getting closer to the issue. This leads us to the question that we are really trying to grapple with: '*How* does God draw us?' The fact of the matter is that every Christian believes in some form of divine election, the question is what *kind* of election? What's more, how much ability does man have to respond to the gospel call?

Traditionally in Christian theology there has been two major camps: those who believe in *conditional* election, and those who believe in *absolute* election. By 'conditional election' we mean that a person's election is 'conditioned' upon God looking down the corridor of time and seeing whether or not the person in question would 'accept' him when presented with the gospel message. God thus elects based on what that person will do. Specifically, if God sees that that person comes to faith in Christ, he puts his imprimatur on them and they become 'elect'.

By 'absolute' or 'unconditional' election we mean that God chose to save certain people based on nothing they would do, but only for God's glory and for his purposes. This decision by God was made outside of time before the universe began. God therefore has purposed to save these people. More importantly, there is a covenant within the Godhead to carry out this salvific plan via the atoning work of Christ *in* time and within a certain geographic area.

Those who over the years have rejected the concept of unconditional election do not have a problem with the general concept of election. What they really seem to have a problem with is the effects of sin, namely: *How did The Fall and sin impact man's ability to see spiritual reality?* Is man simply impaired by the action of Adam's transgression, or is he stone, cold dead?

We can personify these two concepts by turning them into two different men: one of them has had his leg amputated due to a serious accident; the other has had a massive heart attack, died — and is now embalmed and lying in a casket. We now ask both men to walk across the room, touch the wall on the opposite side and walk back.

Now, the amputee has some trouble due to his condition; he stumbles and falls at first as he attempts to cross the room. Finally, he gets up and hops. Breathless, he finally makes it back to his chair where he collapses in exhaustion.

Our eyes now turn to our heart attack victim in the coffin. There does not seem to be any enthusiasm to do the task at hand as he simply lies there. Unhappy with this turn of events, we go over to the coffin and vigorously try to convince him to snap out of it. We reason, cajole, insist — and finally yell. We do all these things to no avail.

Thus, the person who believes in conditional election sees it as that man without a leg; hampered, impaired, but still very much alive and able to perform certain tasks.

Those holding to unconditional election see the situation

as that man embalmed in the casket; dead, immovable and unresponsive.

Now to our last question in this segment: Which view more perfectly squares with scripture? It is our hope in the following pages we will answer this question.

2.
Some Historical Perspectives

Nothing in time happens in a void; everything that transpires in society has some kind of historical precedent. This is especially true in the church. The issue of God's sovereignty is certainly not a new issue. It has not flashed on the scene suddenly without warning. It has been around a long time and has been debated from the start.

One of the major problems in the evangelical world today is ignorance of church history. Many in the church do not know where they have come from or where they are going in regard to doctrinal issues. They have not investigated the Great Councils, the major players, the critical issues, the great heresies and the great triumphs of the Faith. Hence, when deep issues are discussed, many a Christian will think that they are responding in concord with God's Word, when in fact their gas tank is filled with emotion and opinion.

Sad to say, this is especially true with most 'Bible believing' Christians. Many could not give you the time period in which The Reformation took place, or the major issues that sparked it. That is why to discuss the issue at hand without any background elements would be foolishness.

Note that this is not a book about history, but history must have its due if we are to precede any further. What we will attempt to do is to simply lay down some basic groundwork so that we can reference what our forefathers have said on the issue.

3.
The Mighty Spark

There is no doubt that the Protestant Reformation was one of the greatest events in human history. Martin Luther, for all his off centre ways, was used mightily by God to shake off the yoke of Romanism. During the Middle Ages the Catholic Church had grown tremendously in power and prestige. This power reached its zenith with a document issued by Pope Boniface VIII in 1302 called the *Unam Sanctum*. Basically this document declared that, not only are all common people subject to the Roman pontiff, but worldly rulers as well. A national ruler who therefore opposed the Pope risked excommunication. Part and parcel of this declaration was the basic Roman Catholic belief that Christ by His death purchased a giant pool of merit. Saints and martyrs who died also added to this salvific pool. Catholicism therefore taught that only the church, i.e., the Catholic Church, could dispense grace from this pool via the sacraments.

Thus, the Catholic church proper held the keys to salvation. This belief was summarized in the Latin phrase, *Extra Ecclesium nulla Salvus*. That is, 'Outside the Church, No salvation.'

By the early sixteenth century the Catholic Church was a madhouse of corruption. Attempts to reform it from the inside were futile. The Reformation was in the wings just waiting to happen. When Martin Luther nailed his ninety-five theses to the Wittenberg door, the sound of the hammer hitting the nail could be heard all through Europe, and the Reformation was on its way.

Luther had been led by the Holy Spirit to see that man is saved by grace, and grace alone. He could go to Christ directly for forgiveness, rather than to a priest, church or sacrament. Luther was also led to believe that the concept of 'free will' was a myth: the only thing man was free to do was sin. He saw man's will as in total bondage to sin. Indeed, his book *Bondage of the Will* outlined Man's hopeless condition.

During this period there was a great running debate between Luther and a brilliant Catholic humanist named Erasmus. Ironically, Erasmus had written a book entitled, *On The Freedom of the Will* to which Luther's book was a reply. In his book, Erasmus stated:

> I admit that many different views about free choice have been handed down from the ancients about which I have, as yet, no fixed conviction, except that I think there to be a *certain power of free choice* [Emphasis added].

Anyone reading Erasmus' book would quickly see, however, that he had very *definite* views about the issue of free will. Indeed, Erasmus was vigorously opposing the Reformation principles regarding man's condition and Christ's unmerited favour.

Erasmus saw man's will as weakened, not extinguished, just like our friend with the amputated leg. Although man is hampered, he still has the will to respond to God under his own power. He can consider the claims of Christ, ponder, do the math — and then make a conscious decision to 'receive' Christ.

If this sounds familiar it should, for this is precisely how the average Evangelical sees the salvation process: Jesus graciously holds out his arms and says, 'Come'! The sinner stops, thinks, weighs the evidence for the claims of Christ, and then 'makes up his mind' whether to respond.

Again, we ask, 'Is *this* the Gospel?'

If we telescope one hundred years from Luther's time, we find ourselves in a Europe that was, for the most part, solidly in the unconditional election camp. The reader must clearly understand this; evangelists were not running through the Rhine Valley or the Alps pleading with people to 'accept Christ as your personal Lord and Saviour.' No, Europe had a faith solidly grounded on the principles of the Reformation save, of course, for the Roman church.

At that time a man by the name of Jacob Arminius rejected the entire concept of unconditional election, although for most of his life, he had defended the doctrine. As a professor at Leiden University in the Netherlands, he had taken up an in depth study of the Early Church Fathers. The result of this study was his conclusion that the great men of the first five centuries of the church believed in free will. He thus felt to declare that man cannot accept or reject salvation freely demeaned God's plan of salvation, and Man, who is made in the image of God. Like Erasmus, his conclusion was that man's will was impaired, not eliminated.

His views quickly caught on with his students, and thence out into the churches of Europe. Shortly after his death, his followers issued a document that became known as the *Remonstrance of 1610*, because they were 'remonstrating', or rebuking the concept of unconditional election. In this document, and in later more explicit writings, the Arminians, as they were called, taught an election based on *foreseen* faith. That is to say, God looked down the corridor of time and elected some individuals based on what *they* would do when presented with the gospel, rather than God electing some based on *His* will.

They encapsulated their views as follows:

- Partial Depravity – Man's will is impaired, but not destroyed; he can accept or reject the gospel freely.

- Conditional Election – God elects individuals based on foreseen faith

- Universal Atonement – Jesus died and atoned for the sins of every man, woman and child without exception.

- Resistible Grace – The call of the Holy Spirit to repentance can be resisted.

- Falling from Grace – It is possible for a truly redeemed person to fall from grace and lose their salvation.

We spoke earlier of synergism, a joining together of God and man in order to attain salvation. This is precisely what the aforementioned points boil down to. Man and God meet across the table like business partners, shake hands, and reason things out. In the final analysis, it is man who 'makes a decision'. Again, the crux of the matter is the effects of the Fall. Does man have this power of decision in regard to spiritual matters?

The reply to the Arminians came in the form of the Synod of Dort held in the city of Dordrecht, Netherlands, between 1618-19. Once again, remember that the belief in unconditional election was the prevailing view in Europe at the time. The synod was responding to what it felt were heresies *boldly entering into the church of Jesus Christ.*

To the modern day Evangelical, this may be hard to hear. In seventeenth century Europe, the idea that man made 'a decision' for Christ, or 'walked the aisle' to 'receive Jesus' was unthinkable; it was considered contrary to all of the teaching of Christ and the New Testament.

Although the Synod of Dort was national in nature, it also had an international character, as it welcomed twenty-six delegates from eight foreign countries. The five principles brought forth by the synod were a reflection of deeply held convictions based on the clear teachings of the New Testament. They would come to be known as *The Five Points of Calvinism*. Note that John Calvin, the great Geneva reformer, had been dead for decades at the drafting of this document. However, it was the scriptural exegesis that he championed that inspired the members of the synod to identify him with their conclusions.

The 'Five Points' are summarized thus:

- Total Depravity – Because of the Fall, man is unable by his own will to respond to the Gospel.

- Unconditional Election – God elects men to salvation based on His own sovereign will, *not* man's.

- Limited Atonement – Christ died to redeem the *elect only*; He did not die for all without exception.

- Irresistible Grace – The effectual call of the Holy Spirit cannot be resisted. All the elect will come to salvation.

- Perseverance of the Saints – The elect can never lose their salvation and will endure until the end.

We see from the above that the synod hammered home the idea that salvation is totally and completely the work of the triune God: the Father chose a people, the Son died for them, and the Holy Spirit makes Christ's death effective by bringing the elect to faith and repentance, thereby causing them to willingly obey the gospel. Thus God, not man, determines who will be the recipients of salvation.

Later on we will discuss some other historical elements that directly relate to the issue of God's sovereignty and man's will. What we have done is simply to lay some basic framework into which this discussion can be placed.

Since we now have some historical content as a reference point, we can move on to the subject at hand. As we stated at the beginning, there are many scriptures that can be appealed to by both sides. However, rather than forming a checklist, our goal is to get to the core, the essence, of the issue by looking at the themes in scripture from selected texts.

4.

The Darkening Effects

Christians who reject the decree of predestination as outlined by traditional Calvinists, really don't have a problem with the doctrine itself (although they may not know it). What they really have a problem with is the effects of sin on men and women due to Adam's fall. We have asked it before, and we will continue to ask it: *Is man maimed, or is he dead, spiritually speaking?*

We can take as our starting point many different passages of scripture. Logically speaking, you would expect that we would immediately go to Genesis and examine what happened in the garden. But that is not our starting line. Rather, we will go to the apostle Paul's *magnum opus*, the book of Romans. In particular, Romans 5:12-21. As with all passages and themes that we will attempt to examine, the reader would do well to open the Bible and carefully read over these verses a number of times.

Now, admittedly, this passage is perhaps the most complicated in all of the New Testament, indeed, perhaps in the entire Bible. So why start here and confuse the issue? Actually we really only want to grasp one verse, and one concept. The verse we want to deal with is 5:12, and the concept is the impact of sin.

The verse reads as follows:
Therefore, just as through one man sin entered the world, and death through sin, and so death spread to all men, because all sinned ... (NASB)

Perhaps when you were a child you chased a friend or sibling through the house until he or she dashed into a room and tried to close the door on you. But you stuck your foot in the doorway, and after some grunting and pushing, burst your way into the room. This is the mind picture you should have when reading this passage: Sin got its foot in the door, burst through — and did its damage. Sin now runs rampant through the human race. Adam's sin had a definite effect: death.

You may ask, 'What does it mean, though, that we *all* sinned?'

In theological terms, Adam is viewed in two ways; as the 'federal head' of humanity, or as the 'organic head'. In the 'federal' view, we are all pictured as being there with Adam when he sinned, and thus share in the guilt; we would have done the same had we been given the choice. In the 'organic view' we actually carry the sin of Adam in our bodies, as we are his progeny. We are 'rubber stamped', if you will, with his sin. Either way, the results are the same, namely, that death has spread to all men. Clearly, when this passage speaks of 'death', the reference is both to a literal and figurative death. We literally die, that is, our bodies will at some point in time cease to function, and we spiritually 'die' in that we 'cannot hear' God's truth and are under His wrath.

The Darkening Effects

The theological term for this is the *Noetic effects of sin*. That is to say, the darkening of our spiritual consciousness, making us unable and unwilling to hear, receive and act upon spiritual truth.

It cannot be stressed enough that in scripture *sin equals death*. What are the attributes of a dead person? They are totally unresponsive as they are no longer in the world of the living, and have no consciousness whatsoever regarding the physical universe.

This line of thinking is easily transposed to the spiritual realm as regards the proclamation of the gospel. If we are dead in our sins, if by Adam's fall sin entered the world and therefore death, how is it that man can have the intuition to hear and understand the profound truths of God's plan of salvation? The answer is, he cannot.

This identical theme is found in 1 Corinthians 15:22, where we are told, ' … in Adam all die …' The text does not say, 'some die', but that '*all* die'. The second half of this verse is quite significant: '… even so in Christ *all* shall be made alive' (NKJV). What we immediately notice from the entirety of this verse is the interesting way the word 'all' is used. In the first half, there is no doubt that the word 'all' means 'everybody without exception'. But does that hold true for the second half? The obvious conclusion is that it does not. For if we take the second half of this verse at face value, the implication would be that the entire world would be saved — everyone without exception — and, scripturally, that is impossible.

We already see from the aforementioned, and we will develop this further, that all men and women are spiritually dead in Adam. We also see, however, that the second use of 'all' cannot mean everybody, and must refer to a select group of people. The question is *how* are these people 'made alive'?

If we move to 1 Corinthians 15:45, we see that Adam is called a 'living soul' whereas the 'last Adam', Christ, became a 'life-giving spirit'. Here we have the contrast between the 'First Adam' and the 'Second Adam'. Adam produced death and sin while Christ produced life. The heirs of Adam, the human race, cannot produce life (i.e., 'spiritual life') in that they are 'dead' and unresponsive to the gospel. They need an external force to change all that. That force is a move by God Himself. Keep in mind that Christ died while we were 'still helpless' (Rom. 5:6). That helplessness continues on in the human race; we are unable to help ourselves, and are unable to come to Christ. Moreover, we naturally *hate* the gospel message, for it speaks directly to our condition.

Adam miserably failed the test God put before him, Christ triumphantly passed the test and produced the fruit of regeneration. Nothing that man can do will make him righteous. Indeed, men and women refuse to be righteous because their deeds are evil and they refuse to listen.

Man, therefore, in his Adamic state, suffering from the Noetic effects of sin, has absolutely no interest in the saving grace of Christ.

5.
Just How Depraved Am I?

In the classic musical *West Side Story*, there is a scene where one of the hoodlums proclaims, 'Hey, I'm depraved because I'm deprived!' When we speak in spiritual terms, the opposite is true; we are deprived *because* we are depraved. That is, we are deprived of spiritual understanding because we are lost in sin.

But just how depraved are we? Are we capable of any good?

First, when the Bible speaks of our depravity, it is not saying that we are incapable of good acts. Certainly, most of us would gladly help an elderly lady across the road rather than knocking her to the pavement. We are not as bad as we are truly capable of being all the time. The problem is made clear when we contrast our *vertical* and *horizontal* relationships.

Our horizontal relationships are those with family, friends, co-workers and even strangers who cross our path in life. On this level, we are capable of understanding and love. By vertical, we mean our relationship with the Godhead, and this where the trouble starts. There is no way that men and women can have a right relationship with God apart from Jesus Christ. Men and women may know how to relate to their horizontal relationships, but have no idea how to relate to God. Ecclesiastes 9:3 remind us that 'the hearts of the sons of men are full of evil, and insanity is in their hearts throughout their lives. Afterwards they go to the dead.' This does not sound promising, and we should be quick to agree that a madman cannot make very sound decisions. So why should we think that men and women can 'decide' for Jesus?

While we all may have some level of discernment, that discernment is a perversion of its truest form: spiritual enlightenment. From the very beginning of our lives, we fail to see true reality. That is why David in Psalm 51:5 said: 'Behold, I was brought forth in iniquity, And in sin my mother conceived me.' David was not questioning the morality of his mother, or saying that the act of intercourse was sinful. Rather, he was saying that we are born into the world as sinners. That cute little baby in the crib is far from innocent. Do babies need to be taught how to cry when they do not get their way?

The argument is not that men and women are incapable of doing *natural* good, it's that they are incapable of doing *spiritual* good, namely, 'coming to Christ'. In the natural realm, we can feed the poor, love our spouse, pay for our daughter's wedding and campaign to stop the over fishing of herring. But we cannot see through the veil of sin to spiritual truth — apart from election, that is.

It is in the basic nature of men and women that when faced with a decision, our inclination is to take the path of least resistance. Whatever seems easier, whatever seems more pleasing; whatever satisfies the senses is the object we choose. Indeed, the actions of Adam and Eve certainly make this obvious to us.

In Genesis 3:6, we see these sensual instincts at work. The proscriptions that God had given the mother and father of the human race were quickly swept aside as the senses took over. We are told that Eve saw 'that the tree was good for food and that it was pleasing to the eyes … ' It is amazing how we humans are seduced by what looks good, and may in fact be good, but may not be the appropriate thing to have at the time.

We often increase our folly by justifying our actions intellectually. Eve not only liked what she saw, but said to herself that the tree would 'make one wise.' The literal Hebrew here reads, 'full of discernment'. But did we not just say that our discernment is perverted apart from God's will? The combination, however, of good looks and false intellectual back flips overrides all the warning signs.

Noting this, how is it that man could, in any real sense and at any real time, discern between worldly enticements and the perfect will of God? A Christian who holds that men and women are completely 'free to choose' must answer this question without equivocation.

The 'free will' advocate may immediately protest that what we are left with is a human race void of any will whatsoever, that we are all automatons or puppets on a giant stage, and that God is playing some kind of horrible game. This is simply not the case. Scripture is quite clear that men and women have a will that is very active, but it is active doing every kind of evil.

The question before us is: has man's character changed in any positive fashion since the beginning of time? Had not God said regarding man, ' ... every intent of the thoughts of his heart was only evil continually'? Where, then, has the change in perception and discernment occurred in the minds and hearts of men?

6.

A Living Will

To those who would charge that to believe God chooses who will be saved and who will not makes a mockery of the salvation process, our reply is that man is indeed free. We do not argue this. Man's will is very free and very active. But this freedom is not inclined toward God. It is a freedom that desires its own satisfaction and that exalts itself above God's will.

Traditional Calvinists do not believe that man does not have a will. Rather, they believe that man left to his own devices will *never* come to Christ without the direct intervention of the Holy Spirit. Let us be clear about what is being said here, for the free will believer may be quick to agree with this statement.

We are not saying that the Holy Spirit beckons and that everybody is on an equal plane as to whether to believe or not. As we have seen, this cannot be, for man will always choose darkness rather than light (John 3:19). When the Holy Spirit calls to the reprobate, they will not take heed; they will categorically reject the gospel. However, in the case of the elect, they will graciously open their hearts and throw themselves upon the mercy of the cross. This will happen because God has purposed it to happen. The reprobate man or woman will stand guilty. You may immediately protest, 'But they could not do otherwise. How could they be held accountable?' We answer: 'Because of sin! Because they are "in Adam" and must face the consequences: death.'

We have seen very clearly that man is not born into this world as a *tabla rasa*, a blank slate upon which either good or evil can be written. He is born a sinner in total rebellion to God, and is quickly led away by his own lusts (James 1:14). It is not that man *will not* come to Christ of his own free will, but rather that he simply *cannot* come. Man does not have the spiritual equipment to 'decide' for Jesus.

In the book of Romans, Paul really closes the door on the concept that man is still able to 'decide' spiritually after the fall. Frankly, one is hard pressed to understand how any Christian can proclaim man's 'free will' in regard to salvation after even a cursory reading of chapter three (vv. 10-18, in particular). Here, Paul declares that none are righteous (v.10), that no man or woman does anything that is good (v.12); and that no one fears God (v.18). Based on this, what decision can man make except toward his own desires and lusts?

Remember, man's will is not dead; in fact, it is quite active plotting, scheming, coveting, etc. The curious thing is that man, at times, has insights into his condition, and yet plows ahead in his ever increasing desire to sin. The building of the tower of Babel shows this quite clearly. Many Christians simply view this passage of scripture as a quaint story of man's rebellion. However, it is much, much more — and it reveals man's fully active will. That will is, as we have stated, not active at all for good, but is determined to have its own way apart from God, and in direct contradiction to God.

In Genesis 11:1-9, we first see a world that is of 'the same language and the same words' (v. 1). This does not simply mean that the post-deluvian population simply spoke the same language. It also carries with it the idea that they thought the same way also; that they were united in some cultural way. Notice that in the second verse of this passage we are told '... it came about as they journeyed east ... '. They were clearly moving together as one, and we can safely assume that they were of the same mindset.

In verse four we see that, acting as a unit, they decide to build a city and a tower whose 'top will reach into heaven ... '. This is simply an Hebraicism that means something that is 'exceedingly high'. However, one cannot escape the spiritual symbolism involved.

Reading through this entire event, several things become clear to us:

1. They *knew* exactly what they were doing.
2. They *understood* their condition.
3. They attempted to *remove God* from the equation.

Had not God told the post-deluvians to re-populate the earth? This would entail spreading out across the globe in various directions and in various groups. But there is power in numbers, and to split off in to several traveling groups would diminish that power. Hence, to stay in one place, and to build a large city would not only maintain their power, but enhance it as well.

So it is clear that they knew their estate, and outright refused to follow the command of Almighty God. In fact, the high tower was more than a symbol. It may have been intended to be some sort of astrological observatory, in which the occupants of the city could chart the stars, divine future events and act as a counterfeit deity.

This idea is reinforced by a clear declaration by Jehovah God Himself. Upon watching the proceedings on earth below, his comment on their possible success in verse six is quite chilling: ' ... and now *nothing* which they purpose to do will be impossible for them' [Emphasis added]. You see the plans and schemes of men can be quite ingenious. Apart from God's divine intervention and sovereignty in all of history, man *would* be as bad as he possibly could be. This entire event shows that man's will is alive and well — and quite active. Man's desire, however, is not to obey God's commands in order to be under his protection, but, in fact, to rebel against God. Indeed, man's will is to find a way to become greater than God.

The desire to find the 'fountain of youth' in medical research, to attempt to clone human beings, to control climate; and to decide when babies in the womb are to be terminated are all witnesses to this fact. Man has an insatiable lust for power. It may manifest itself in different ways, but the end result is always the same; rebellion against God and His statutes. More to the point, because of this fact, man, given the choice, *would never* and *could never* 'choose' Christ.

Everything that we have studied so far is interconnected.

Nothing that we have said is stated as a fact apart from the whole. When studying the Bible, we must be painfully aware of this. To atomize texts of scripture and set them apart from the great continuum of God's Word is to do the Lord himself a great disservice. The salvation plan of God is one that is carefully and painstakingly detailed in His Word. Just like the precious gift it is, we must unpack it carefully lest we break pieces off or fail to see its full beauty. Certainly one of the most beautiful things about salvation is that man can claim absolutely no part in it — nothing! He can neither attain to salvation himself, nor add to the finished product. But the Christian can and must do one thing: He or she must bask in the knowledge that a loving and sovereign Creator has chosen them to be an heir of salvation, and now holds them firmly in his benevolent grip.

7.
'When You're Dead, You're Dead!'

We have often heard unbelievers use this phrase in regard to man's ultimate fate. The idea is that there is no consciousness beyond the grave. In this, the unbeliever is making a dreadful and eternal error. However, even unbelievers can come up with a spark of truth, for in this phrase we see our basic spiritual condition, namely that we are dead in our sins. Men and women are dead to the call of the gospel. Just like our heart attack victim in the coffin, we are unresponsive; we do not partake in discussions or debate ideas and concepts in this condition. Once a person has expired, doctors are not sitting around pondering how to bring the patient back. They may have revived the patient momentarily, but if they keep getting a flat line on the monitor, it's over.

For the human race, any hope of responding to a loving God under their own steam is over. It has been over since Adam's transgression, and man's character has not improved with time, no matter what social evolutionists claim. Christians should be the first to see this, but many fail to. We believe that all must be on an equal footing. We are outraged when our government enacts laws that we think are 'unfair'. We loathe discrimination in any form, and are constantly chanting our mantra 'equal rights'.

It is no wonder, then, that when scripture speaks of God

having chosen us based on nothing that we would do or can do, there is a fuss. But the fact of the matter is we are dead. Our spiritual ears are deaf. There is simply no point of connection between the salvation plan of the Bible and the human consciousness apart from divine intervention. While it is true that general revelation renders us 'without excuse' (Rom. 1:20), we are vehemently opposed to God's solution to man's problem because it does not involve our will, but His.

If there is any theme in the New Testament that is clearer than day, it's the concept of our 'deadness' to the call of the gospel. Conversely, if there is any other theme that is just as clear, it is God's electing grace. These two concepts form the bookends of scripture; they hold the thread of redemption together.

There are a handful of significant scriptures that speak to these issues. What we would like to do here is look at those that talk of our inability. Once we grasp this, our understanding of God's redemptive plan becomes more focused and easier to comprehend.

The book of Ephesians stands as a monument to God's election plan and the unity of his work in the church. The first chapter is chock full of his election plan. We are told that he 'chose us in Him before the foundation of the world' (v.4), that 'He predestined us to adoption as sons … ' (v. 5), that 'He lavished upon us' the riches of His grace (v. 8); and that we 'have obtained an inheritance, having been predestined according His purpose …' (v.11). What could be clearer?

Within one chapter of scripture the Lord of the universe sweeps aside man's 'free will' and replaces it with his own — thankfully.

In chapter two, Paul meditates on the Christian's former dead state, and his newness in Christ as it relates to the church. The first verse of this chapter is handled differently by various translations. The King James reads, 'And you *hath he quickened*, who were dead in trespasses and sins.' The words 'hath he quickened' are in italics in the KJV because they are an insertion by the translators. The original Greek does not contain these words. The NASB has the best rendering of this verse: 'And you were dead in your trespasses and sins … ' This is a direct and blunt statement. We were dead; we were not able to respond in any way. Verse four, however, tells us that God is rich in mercy toward the elect. This leads us to verse five where we are told that God 'even when we were dead in our transgressions, made us alive together with Christ (by grace you have been saved)… '

It is evident that the whole salvation process is God toward man, not vice versa. Many times the gospel will be presented in such a way as to make it appear that God has made the first step, or that he has done all that he can, and now the sinner must 'do something'. Usually, the sinner is told that Christ is holding out the gift of salvation and he or she must now 'receive it'. In some sense this is true because God holds all men and women accountable. However, our salvation in Christ is based solely on the electing grace of God, not on our ability to reason. Hence, this method of evangelism, where one is asked to 'walk the aisle' and 'take the free gift' is faulty, unbiblical — and even heretical.

A verse that will be appealed to here by the free will advocate is John 1:12: 'But as many as have received Him, to them He gave the right to become children of God ... ' The problem here is that whenever this verse is quoted, it is quoted in isolation, for verse 13, the very next verse, explains what this 'reception' is all about: 'who were born not of blood, *nor of the will of the flesh, nor of the will of man, but of God'* [Emphasis added].

This is precisely why we are not 'stacking' verses to prove our point, for a single verse may not fully explain itself. We must always look at the entire passage in context. In business, as the saying goes, it's 'location, location, location'. When studying God's Word, it's 'context, context, context'!

Colossians 2:13 is another important verse that has almost identical language to Ephesians 2:4-5: 'And when you were dead in your transgressions and the uncircumcision of your flesh, He made you alive together with Him ... ' There is no mistaking that the action being taken is on behalf of the sinner by God. There is no indication that the object of this regenerative power is 'doing something.' Nor can we by eisegesis read this into the text. In fact, the end of the verse reads: '... having forgiven us all our transgressions ... ' The Greek word used for 'forgiven' here has as its root the idea of 'grace'; viz., 'utilizing grace' or 'given grace'. There is no intimation here that there is some sort of symbiotic relation-ship going on between God and man. Man is not pictured here as cogitating on certain verities, and then making some kind of free will decision. God here is working upon the object, and that object is man. That is not to say that man does not re-spond, but this response is based upon the faith that is given to him.

We must restate again and again that men and women simply are not equipped to respond in a positive fashion to the gospel. This is unequivocally stated in Romans 8:7, where we are told that, ' ... the mind set on the flesh is *hostile toward God*; for it does not subject itself to the law of God, for it is not even able to do so ... ' [Emphasis added]. The words 'not even able to do so' can be translated from the Greek, 'does not/neither has the power'. The force of this statement is overwhelming: we are powerless to affect a change in our spiritual situation. It is God — and all God, that does the changing. Man claims nothing in the salvific work of Christ.

Man is not a 'free agent', a neutral entity trying to decide between good and evil. Quite the contrary, man is a slave of the devil and sin, and it is God who grants man the grace to 'come to his senses' (cf. 2 Tim. 2:25-26). All of the healings that we see Jesus performing in the gospels can be taken on two levels. The first is the obvious physical healing; the second is Jesus directly entering the lives of people to heal them from their sin. Leprosy, blindness, lameness and the like are all metaphors for our fallen and powerless state.

Man in his 'natural', or unredeemed state, may know that there is a 'god', some *kind* of 'god'; but cannot discern the *true* and *living* God. More to the point, man cannot comprehend a salvation plan as specific and unique as that outlined in the Bible. Even reading the words of Scripture do not do him any good. His spirit must be 'made alive' in order for those words to mean anything and impact his life.

Again, the 'natural man' is dead to spiritual truth. In 1 Corinthians 2:14, this idea is stated quite succinctly:

But a natural man does not accept the things of the Spirit of God; for they are foolishness to him, and he cannot understand them, because they are spiritually appraised. (NASB)

The natural man, being spiritually dead, relies on the 'logic' of the world. This 'logic' will lead him to believe, as we have earlier stated, that there is something ridiculous about the vicarious death of Christ. Even if he buys into the concept of someone dying on his behalf, he will instantly seek to inject his own will in the matter. Thus, someone may have died for him, but he will now insist that by his own volition he completes the process. This is a man-centered response. But this is precisely the way the gospel is presented from pulpits all across the country, to the church's shame.

The Christian must delete from his or her lexicon the terms 'receive', 'accept', 'grab hold of', 'take the gift', etc., and replace them with the term 'trust'. That is what we are doing

41

when we become Christians. We are trusting in the atoning work of Christ; we are making Him our Lord. We are saying that we deserve hell and damnation and don't really understand how he could love us. But we trust. This is the essence of the gospel and the way things work in God's plan.

8.
Election: The Word That Brings Comfort

When we come to trust in Jesus Christ, we are in a sense made uncomfortable. That is, we must now face a world that is hostile to our ideas, because we have put away our old way of thinking and 'put on Christ'. We now think like a Christian, and most of the time we will be at odds with the prevailing worldview. Of course, there is another side to the Christian life, and that is the one that brings comfort, namely, our election.

Perhaps you have never thought of the Christian life this way. There is no doubt about it, however, that election brings comfort. There are those who feel quite the opposite for they view the doctrine of election as an unfair, and even inhumane, concept of salvation. But we have already seen that the natural man is like the proverbial dog chasing his tail; around and around he goes, but does not accomplish anything. Human logic can never aspire to the lofty things of God. So we must trust. Sometimes we don't realize what a wonderful thing it is to trust someone fully. When we put our full trust in someone, anxiety melts away. We can relax. We know that that person is working for our good. We also know that whatever action they take, it will be the right action. So it is with Our Lord. His decisions are always the right decisions. His thoughts for us are always good thoughts, his plans always good plans.

As the book of Jeremiah puts it, these plans and thoughts are for 'welfare and not for calamity to give you a future and a hope' (29:11). We must believe that this is true, or our faith is in vain.

The apostle Paul reminds us of the great comfort that we have in election. In 2 Thessalonians 2:13-17, he gives us much fertile ground to plant our trust. First, we are told that Christians should always give thanks to God because 'God has chosen you from the beginning for salvation through sanctification by the spirit and faith in the truth.'

Our gratitude to God is grounded in our election. God chose to save us from the beginning. This fact should fill our hearts with joy and thankfulness. There was never a doubt that we would become children of God. The salvation plan of God is not based on entropy. That is, it is not a random process whereby Christ made you 'saveable' by His death, and now it's up to you to make 'the right decision'.

Many picture the atonement of Christ as a supernatural key that unlocks the gates of heaven. Man had been shut out and lost the key, but Christ opened the gates and now asks you to follow Him. Yet one more time, we must protest that this is *not* the teaching of Christ or the New Testament. The death of Christ was specific in that it was one thousand per-cent effective; all that Christ came to save will be saved; his plan cannot be thwarted.

The nexus of the issue is God's control of the universe. Will things take place in the span of time and space that God cannot control? Should we believe that God chooses not to control certain things? If we say yes to either of these statements we run the risk of believing in a 'god' who is not fully in control, and who allows the creatures to take the helm. We can give God all the glory, however, that such is not the case.

At this point it is important to look at the next verse of this passage for it tells us how we came to so great a comfort. We are told that Christ 'called you through our gospel ...' Christians came to faith in Christ by the hearing of the gospel. We are commanded to witness to the lost. This fact must be highlighted lest we again fall into a thinking pattern that concludes we are all part of a divine marionette show and that God sits and pulls the strings while we day dream. The contrary is true: we are commanded to preach the Word to every creature and be active in the proclamation of truth.

It is interesting to note that when Christ gives the Great Commission in Matthew 28:18-20, there is a direct and organic connection between the command to preach the gospel and the omnipotence of Christ. Jesus claimed that 'all authority' had been given to Him (v.18), and therefore we can make disciples in his name (v. 19). His conclusion is a word of comfort for the disciples and all future evangelists: 'I am with you always, even to the end of the age.'

So we are not only assured that our salvation was determined before time but, additionally, that as we go forth with the gospel message others who are elect will also turn to Christ. Our efforts are guaranteed fruit!

Let's return to 2 Thessalonians chapter two and look at the last two verses of our passage. In 2:16 it is clear that our comfort in Christ is not something to strive for; we already have it. Paul tells his readers that God the Father has 'loved us and given us eternal comfort and good hope by grace...' We might want to reflect on where we would be if the comfort part depended on us. If it did, we would simply be part of the self-help, psychoanalytic crowd of our day. There is no doubting that this mentality has deeply infested the church. We want to feel good about ourselves and put our self-esteem on a pedestal. But we are grievous sinners who must look each day to the Saviour who has given us, not self-esteem, but comfort in him. The work of Christ has a practical effect as we read in the last verse of our passage that God himself will 'comfort and strengthen' our hearts so that we will be successful in 'every good work and word'.

You see our election has an outward manifestation in that we are to show our gratefulness by our love for the brethren and the lost. There must be fruit on the tree, but it is not a sombre and weathered tree, rather a joyful one. This joy and practical outworking of election is the answer to the naysayers who claim election removes the heart of the gospel. Indeed, election *is* the heart of the gospel.

In 2 Timothy 2:10, the apostle Paul reminds us that he endures 'all things for the sake of those who are chosen ...' He endures because there is a God that has a specific people whom he came to earth to save. Jesus Christ did not die for a theoretical, faceless mass of people. We are told plainly in Matthew 1:21 that Jesus 'will save *His people* from their sins' [Emphasis added].

Who are Jesus' people? Those whom the Father has elected from before the foundation of the world are His people. Jesus' mission had an objective. That objective was not to make certain things 'possible', i.e., the theoretical salvation of those who 'make a decision' for him, but to secure the salvation of the chosen.

If you have followed our line of thinking so far, you will clearly see that God uses the chosen to *call out* the chosen. That is, God calls out his own, equips them with the Word, and then they in turn preach the gospel to others from which the elect will be called out. What could illustrate this better or be more dramatic in doing so than the conversion of Paul.

In Acts 9:1-9, we read of the incredible 'Saul into Paul' conversion. There are several important things that should strike us as we read this text. The first of these is right at the beginning in the first two verses. Those who believe in 'free will' must be confronted with this story and what it has to say regarding the issue of character change in men and women. We read in the first verse that Saul was, 'still breathing threats and murder against the disciples of the Lord ...' We do not see in this verse a Saul who, on the way to Damascus, is thinking, 'Hmmm ... maybe I'm wrong about this Jesus. You know, I've been doing some soul searching after hearing what his disciples have to say about him and ... well ... he does seem to fit the profile of Messiah ...' This was not the case with Saul; his heart showed absolutely no change. He was not 'considering the claims of Christ' as many of our free will friends would say. He was not weighing the evidence in order to 'make a decision' for Christ. In fact, it is quite clear that his mind was made up: he wanted to erase every trace of this new cult's teaching and its followers.

The text goes on to say that as Saul journeyed, a light shone from heaven and he was struck to the ground (vs. 3-4). Dear friend, *this* is the picture of salvation. We are going our own way, either oblivious to God, or in outward opposition to God, when suddenly our excuses and defences are struck down. As new Christians, we are then told by the Word of God to 'rise ... and it will be told you what you must do'. We do this as we sit under the preaching of God's truth in a local body.

Saul did nothing as he travelled to Damascus to warrant the grace of God in Christ. Yet, many tell us that we can sort of 'get the ball rolling' as regards our redemptive position. Witness the following selected quotes:

> *By free will one shapes his own life ... As long as freedom has not bound itself definitely to its ultimate good; that is, God ... there is the possibility of choosing good or evil ... The more one does what is good, the freer one becomes ... freedom attains perfection in its acts when directed toward God ... the sovereign Good ...*

The aforementioned quotes were taken from Article 3 of the *Catechism of the Catholic Church*. What exactly is being said here? Basically the teaching goes something like this: You choose to do 'the good'. As you choose to do good acts, you desire to do more good acts. You say to yourself that you are doing these things for God. Therefore, what you are doing is predisposing yourself to the grace of God, so that, when the Holy Spirit draws you, your heart will be opened to the truth and you will 'accept' Jesus.

This all sounds logical and quite wonderful, but it assumes that man has the seed of good to respond in the first place. A person may be predisposed to do good works, but all the good works in the world will not make them righteous before God.

Nowhere is man's hopeless state and God's sovereignty better encapsulated than in the historical narrative of the raising of Lazarus in John chapter eleven. Here we see the frail, frame of dust nature of man as opposed to the glorious regenerating power of God; a power of life over death.

In the beginning of this chapter we are told that Lazarus, the brother of Mary, was sick. This was the Mary who had anointed Jesus' feet with ointment. We are also told of Jesus' great love for Mary, her sister Martha and Lazarus. As we read this story, the one thing that should jump off the page at us is Jesus' reaction to Lazarus' illness: He (i.e., Jesus) stayed two more days where he was (v. 6). Now, most of us if we heard that a dear friend was sick, and we were within a reasonably short distance away, would immediately make plans to depart and be with our beloved. Jesus' reaction, therefore, seems a bit odd. We started this chapter by talking about comfort. One of the things that Christians must do when confronted with difficult circumstances or tragedy is to trust. We do not need to understand the situation, or how and when God will relieve us of the pain of same, but we *must* trust. So when we read of Christ prolonging his stay in the area even though a dear friend in another village was gravely ill, we must trust that he had a purpose — and indeed he had.

After two days had passed, Jesus informs the disciples that they were to go to Judea again. The disciples reply that it is a dangerous place; they had just come from there and the Jews had sought to stone Jesus. Why tempt fate? But Christ is the King of the Universe who has entered time and this world to conquer evil, indeed, even death. When Jesus informed the disciples, therefore, that Lazarus had 'fallen asleep' and that he was going to 'wake him', they did not understand. Jesus then plainly tells them that Lazarus is dead and makes yet another seemingly odd statement: He is glad that he was not there. Why? So that they may believe (v.15).

When Jesus arrives at the tomb, he finds that Lazarus had been dead for some four days. He assures Martha that her brother will rise again. Martha replies that she understands; her brother will rise on the last day. Jesus then tells Martha that *he* is the resurrection. You see, we must rely on the power of God only. He and *only* he has the power to make us alive. We are dead.

Jesus then instructs that the stone be rolled away. However, Martha protests that there will be a stench. The King James Version puts it quite graphically: 'Lord, by this time he stinketh …' That is all of us before we are regenerated, we 'stinketh'. We are rotting with sin and have no capability in ourselves to help our condition. Lazarus dead in the tomb is a perfect picture of unredeemed humanity.

When Jesus yelled, 'Lazarus, come forth,' you can be assured that Lazarus did not sit up in the tomb and say to himself, 'Well, I don't know. Should I come out or not? Hmmm … let me think about this for a while!' This may seem like outlandish rubbish, but we can conclude that the believer in man's 'free will' must see this as a definite possibility, for if Lazarus was made alive and his 'free will' was restored, why would he not have such a choice?

So far we have seen that the very language of scripture precludes any concept of man making a 'free will decision for Christ'. We said at the beginning of this book that one could string verses together like pearls to try to prove an argument, but you simply cannot change the meaning of the original language or the specificity of the text.

We will now move on and look at examples of how scripture uses some very specific language when talking about who are the elect and who are not.

9.
Some Very Specific Sheep

Question: When are sheep not really sheep?
Answer: When they decide for themselves where they are going and how they are going to get there.

Sheep are herd animals. That is, they travel in a group, and because they are not, to be kind, very intelligent, they need to be led.

God's Word tells us that we humans, by our very nature, are like sheep. We are not spiritually perceptive because of our fallen status, or to use a common vernacular phrase, we are 'spiritually challenged'. We therefore need to be led. We will either be led by Christ, or by the devil; but we *will* be led.

This all relates to the use of the term 'coming to Christ'. For only Christ's true sheep will follow Him. The master who owns them calls the sheep. The sheep themselves, however, are in no position to decide who their master is; they are not roaming the fields in profound thought about whom they should choose as their shepherd. Rather, the shepherd owns them. He, the master, calls them and they respond because they are his. Christ stated in John 6:37, 'All that the Father gives Me will come to Me.' The Father gives the sheep to Christ. The work of salvation is done in the Godhead, it is not the work of the sheep, nor do the sheep contribute in any way to this work. The sheep are regenerated and then, and only then, do they respond to the call of Christ.

There are two theological terms that must be understood in order to grasp what is going on in the salvation process. The first is the *ordo salutis,* i.e., 'order of salvation', and the other is the *pactum salutis*, or the 'covenant of redemption'.

Simply put, the *ordo salutis* has to do with the *order* in which we are saved. There are two main views regarding this matter. The first states that the sinner considers the claims of Christ, believes them, and makes a 'decision' to 'receive' him. At that moment, the sinner is regenerated and becomes 'born again'. Note that the sinner confesses Christ *before* he or she is regenerated. There are two major problems that should be immediately apparent as one considers this position. First, this model puts men and women in control of when they are saved. It shifts the power to men. The second problem can be framed in the form of a question: How is it that the sinner in question can confess Christ without the indwelling of the Holy Spirit? Indeed, how is it that a person whose spirit is still darkened by the effect of the Fall and sin be 'saved' apart from true spiritual regeneration?

This brings us to the second position that says that the sinner is *first* regenerated and *then* confesses Christ. If you have followed our argument thus far, this is the only true and satisfactory conclusion that can be made, for without the Holy Spirit's regenerating work, we are spiritually dead, immovable and deaf to redemption. One may protest that it *is* the Holy

Spirit who is drawing the sinner in the first example. But there is a great deal of difference between being drawn and actually indwelled. A simple 'drawing' means that the unregenerate man or women moves toward Christ as one would move toward the aroma of a delicious meal. We may love the smell of that meal, but it may still not be to our liking, and thus we do not partake of it. Contrary to this, God lovingly calls out his own, the ones he purposed to save from before the foundation of the world. He does this to glorify himself and to secure a people that will be called by his name. We must therefore put our trust in this merciful God who knows better than any man.

The second term we mentioned was the *pactum salutis.* This is the covenant between Christ and those whom the Father gave him. Since we do not serve a God who does things 'catch-as-catch-can', it is an agreement that was made within the Godhead before the creation of the physical universe. Essentially, this covenant cannot be broken or altered in any way. There is therefore an assurance that those whom Christ came to save will be saved and will persevere. What's more, there is an eternal imputation of righteousness to those that are his.

In simple terms, the free will believer 'asks Jesus into his heart', and then Christ graciously responds to the offer. In the Reformed model, the sinner is first regenerated, and then a profession of faith is made. God in this case is always in control as he works his ultimate plan. In the first view, the ultimate decision is left to men who are like a 'Lazarus' in the tomb pondering whether or not to come out. This assumes, once again, that men and women can decipher true spiritual reality from false, and that they can separate emotions from true biblical repentance. We have already established, however, that those who are 'dead' cannot respond in any way, shape or form to the offer of salvation apart from the regenerating power of Almighty God. This must be as we are sheep who need to return to the Shepherd. It is the shepherd who knows the sheep, calls them out and shows them the way home.

This analogy of sheep and shepherd is clearly delineated in chapter ten of John's gospel. In verse twenty-two we are told that it is the Feast of the Dedication. The Jews take this opportunity to gather about Jesus and badger him as to whether or not he is the promised Messiah. How long will he keep them in suspense? Jesus' reply is more than noteworthy; it is absolutely devastating. He tells the Jews present that he has told them the truth about his identity, but they do not believe. Why do they not believe? Is it because they just have not studied the issue out? Do they just need to lower their defences and give up their prideful ways? Have they have not heard the gospel enough times? No, the reason is '… you are not of My sheep'.

The force of the text is not that these Jews are presently not his sheep, but could someday be. Rather, it is that they will *never* be his sheep. They are not 'his people'; they can never comprehend the gospel message and will remain reprobate.

So we have some very particular language from Jesus himself stating that there are those who will *never* be his sheep. Conversely, there are those that are his sheep and will forever be.

In the very next verse (v.27), Jesus tells us, 'My sheep hear My voice, and I know them, and they follow Me, and I give eternal life to them.' Note that they are his sheep. He gives them eternal life. The power of regeneration is Christ's and Christ's alone. The sheep hear his voice because the Father gave them to Christ before time began.

Salvation is not a hit or miss proposition. Christ does not 'do all he can do' and then hope for the best. He does not hold out the gift of salvation all nicely wrapped so as to attract the sinner like a moth to a flame. Jesus, on the contrary, is the captain of the ship. He calls, regenerates and sustains. The sheep must therefore look to him for all their needs.

When Evangelicals think of the offer of the gospel, far too often they couch it in romantic terms. They see a forlorn Jesus weeping for sinners to come to him, reaching out as people of the world pass by and begging them to 'receive him'. Scripture, however, nowhere substantiates this view. We do not serve a partially sovereign or impotent Saviour. Jesus came to reclaim a people that were lost; a peculiar people — and thus he died for them, and them alone.

What about the universal call of the gospel? First, we can say along with the reformers that it is a sincere call. Yet, many will not come. 'Of course', you may reply, 'they are not the "chosen". So what do you expect?' But scripture is clear that our sin prevents us from coming, and it is sin that will condemn the unbeliever to hell. Often times, we hear from many preachers that God doesn't really want to send anybody to hell. In fact they say God sends no one to hell; people send themselves there. Dear friend, this is an outrage against a Holy God and Our Lord Jesus Christ! It is God alone who saves, and God indeed sends sinners to hell. Why? Because of sin.

In Matthew 11:28 we read what the church has called, 'The Great Invitation'. There is a famous painting by Bloch depicting this verse. It shows Christ holding out His arms as the apostles cling to His robe. This is the mind picture most Christians have when they read this verse. Indeed, it is a beautiful image. 'Come to Me,' our Lord says, 'all who are weary and heavy laden, and I will give you rest.' Surely, Christ is calling to all because he died for all, right? But you must go back one verse in order to properly understand the context. The reader is asked to examine it very carefully:

> *All things have been handed over to me by my Father; and no one knows the Son, except the Father; nor does anyone know the Father, except the Son,* **and anyone to whom the Son wills to reveal Him.**

Clearly, it is Jesus who is in control of revealing spiritual truths to the sinner, and thus regenerating the heart. Moreover, the text clearly indicates that the gospel is hid from the large majority of people in the world. On what basis does Jesus 'reveal the Father'? Simply put, he reveals the Father 'to whom he will'. We do not know why Jesus chooses some and not others, nor can we know. This issue relates once again to the concept of 'fairness'. What is 'fair' to God may not seem 'fair' to us. God, however, is righteous and fair in all his judgements.

In Jesus' 'High Priestly Prayer' (John 17), we do not see Jesus engaged in some kind of universal intercessory prayer. On the contrary, Jesus prays, 'I do not ask on behalf of the world, but of those whom Thou hast given Me; for they are Thine ...' In this text Jesus is not getting all misty eyed over the unbelieving world. He is, rather, praying for the believers *in* an unbelieving world. Jesus is about to die for 'his people,' not the world. The spiritual safety of the elect is his concern, not the mass of reprobates.

We must keep in mind that when the gospel is proclaimed, only the elect will 'hear' it. The reprobate may hear many sermons, and may even come to the point where they can articulate the gospel exactly. However, regeneration is another matter. The gospel is hid to the unelect; they can neither understand nor respond to it.

In chapter thirteen of Matthew's gospel, the disciples come to Jesus and ask him why he speaks in parables (v.10). Jesus tells them, 'To you it has been granted to know the mysteries of the kingdom of heaven, but to them it has not been granted.'

Again, there is a group that are granted to 'hear' and a group to whom the gospel is hidden. In its historical context, Christ speaking in parables was a judgement on the nation of Israel for their rejection of the Messiah who had come. In general soteriology, the 'deafening' of the reprobate is a judgement on an unbelieving world, a world filled with sin that rejects the Gospel of Life.

In verse sixteen of this same chapter, Jesus tells the disciples, 'Blessed are *your eyes* because they see, and *your ears,* for they hear'. Why do they 'hear'? Is it because they have been with Jesus for some time now and have debated the issue of whether or not he is Messiah, and the evidence to them seems clear? Is it because they were born into the world as highly evolved spiritual entities with greater perception than the average person? When the apostle Peter proclaimed in Matthew 16:16 that Jesus was '... the Christ, the Son of the living God,' Our Lord's answer could not have been clearer: '... flesh and blood did not reveal this to you, but My Father who is in heaven.'

It is God who opens the eyes. It is God who reveals spiritual truths. Most importantly, it is God who chooses, not man (John 15:16). Unless we come to the point where we fully believe this, we can never truly understand the gospel or, for that mater, truly love Christ. For if in the final analysis, man chooses and not God, we have then deified man and put human will on the throne. But the Bible is constantly telling us our will is in total bondage to sin. Sin is our master, and whatever pet sins man has he loves and cherishes so as to protect them. In the dark recesses of our souls there are sins that we foolishly believe God knows nothing of, and so we put our best 'Sunday morning' face forward thinking we have deceived all. God, however, shines his search light of truth through the window of our being, and our conscience is stripped of its flimsy shield.

10.
How Effective Was The Cross?

Jesus Christ's appearance on this earth, his incomprehensible incarnation wherein he performed astounding miracles; his suffering and vicarious death on the cross — and his ultimate resurrection to glory and victory over death, all failed miserably. That is the only conclusion one can draw if you believe that man 'decides to get saved'. If Jesus died for every man, woman and child that ever existed, and then gives humanity a 'free will' choice to 'receive him', then the cross was a failure indeed since common man could reject Eternal God.

Throughout the years the church has heard the din of preachers pleading with sinners to come to Christ because, it is thought, Jesus died for all without exception. Jesus, they say, died for you, so how could you possibly turn your back on him? After all, he loves you *so* much!

This romantic view of redemption tugs at our hearts; it just seems so right, so — dare we use the term — just. But is this an accurate view of what the gospel is all about?

The entire matter can be stated thus: 'What did Jesus' death on the cross accomplish?'

Let's be more specific about the matter: Did Jesus make salvation *possible*, or did He actually *purchase* a people? So far in our discussion, this theme has pervaded everything, and rightly so, as it is the core of the gospel. The person who believes in a 'free will' gospel must answer this question, and the answer must jibe with the entirety of the biblical data.

We are often told by many well-meaning clerics that in order to understand God's salvation plan, we must put aside all logic. This is, in part, true. We stated earlier that human logic could never attain to the lofty things of God. However, when the Holy Spirit indwells us, our minds are renewed; we 'put on' the mind of Christ. As such, we can now use logic devoid of human sophistry, and be guided by the light of true science, rather than false. With this firmly in hand, we can look at the cross with spiritual eyes.

Christ took the wrath of God in the place of sinners. When He went to the cross, he took the sinner's every sin. This is where we begin and end in order to understand the vicarious atonement. If the sinner is in bondage (and indeed he is!), and if Christ went to the cross to die for all the sins of that sinner, does it not follow that the sinner in question is freed from his or her sin?

Let's come at this from another angle by asking a very obvious but important question: Is unbelief a sin? Specifically, is not to believe in the vicarious atonement of Christ, his death, resurrection and enthronement at the right hand of God, a sin? We then ask another question with the risk of sounding repetitious: Did Jesus take this sin to the cross? If he took every sin to the cross, he took this one too. This is simple logic. If therefore Jesus took unbelief to the cross, the power of this sin would be broken, and the sinner may freely then believe.

The free will advocate must come up with a refutation of this logic. They must do so in light of what we have established is man's state, namely, his absolute spiritual impotence in making a choice as to whether to trust Christ or not.

There is only one way in which the free will advocate may circumvent this theological schema. They must state boldly that Christ died for all without exception, but somehow gives to all men and women the ability to choose. It is interesting that this idea harkens back to early church history and a great controversy that arose in the fifth century.

At that time a man by the name of Pelagius was preaching outright heresy regarding the nature of man and the redemptive work of Christ. Pelagius was a British layman who fancied himself a theologian. He began to teach that since everything that God creates is good, then man is good also. Since man was created good, Adam's sin did not impair man in any way. Pelagius thus reasoned that Adam made a complete free will choice to disobey God, and that this transgression did not pass to his progeny. Hence, Pelagius did away with the concept of original sin and the collective 'fall' of mankind. Men and women, therefore, could choose to be good and thus attain salvation by their good works. Moreover, Pelagius maintained that man in this life could reach a state of sinless perfection.

The great bishop of Hippo, Augustine, opposed Pelagius. Augustine held to the great Pauline doctrine of salvation by grace alone, which was to be the battle cry of the reformers centuries later. In 529 A.D. the nascent Catholic Church took up this dispute at the Council of Orange. The council roundly trounced Pelagius' teachings in its twenty-five canons. However, in its conclusions the council left the door open to human co-operation with God:

> *According to the catholic faith we also believe that after grace has been received through baptism, all baptized persons have the ability and responsibility, if they desire to labour faithfully, to perform with the aid and co-operation of Christ what is of essential importance in regard to the salvation of their soul. We not only do not believe that any are foreordained to evil by the power of God, but even state with utter abhorrence that if there are those who want to believe so evil a thing, they are anathema.*

The council did not, therefore, exterminate the belief that man can assist in his own salvation. This developed into the doctrine of semi-pelagianism that stated that God gives enough grace to all men and women so that they may 'lift the veil' of original sin brought on by Adam's fall and thus have an equal opportunity to 'decide' for Christ. In later years, this concept, especially in Methodism, became known as 'prevenient grace', or the grace given to all men. It is certainly not over stepping our bounds to say that, although given another acceptable name, it is still the same semi-pelagian heresy wrapped in a new dressing. The really frightening thing about all this is that the majority of Evangelicals in the country holds to this belief and think it is the model of biblical orthodoxy! It is no understatement to say that the church has much to repent of and get right.

When Jesus went to the cross, what was he trying to accomplish? The key word in the aforementioned is 'trying'. Those who believe in a free will gospel must use this word when speaking of God's plan of redemption. They must do so because their model of how God operates allows for the possibility that his will can be thwarted; that man can brush Almighty God off with a stroke of his hand, and leave the Creator whimpering in a corner of the universe mumbling about how much he loves the reprobate.

After Job had experienced the horrors of what life could bring, the verbal barrage of his so-called friends; and the final proclamations of God, his response was altogether in keeping with the rest of revealed Scripture: 'I know that thou canst do all things, And that no purpose of Thine can be thwarted' (42:2). There is a whole lot of theology packed into this statement.

If we believe that Jesus suffered and died for sinners that could reject him, do we not then have a theoretical salvation? This would mean that Jesus saved no one by his vicarious death; he simply made salvation possible. This 'possible' salvation is contingent on man's proclivities. Man has a 'fair chance' of understanding the cross because of prevenient grace. The playing field has been levelled, and humanity can choose or reject Christ. Thus in the Day of Judgement, men and women will have no excuse because they had their chance and 'blew it'. Scripture, however, teaches no such thing.

The ninth chapter of the book of Hebrews presents a challenge to free will advocates. They must explain precisely what Christ has purchased by His vicarious death. We refer specifically to the second half of verse twelve, which states: '... He entered the holy place once for all, having obtained eternal redemption.' Whose 'eternal redemption' did Christ obtain?

First, we need to clarify what the phrase, 'once for all' means. Perhaps it is easier to state what it does *not* mean. It does *not* mean that Christ died for 'all' people. The thrust of the Greek here is that Christ died 'once for all time'. The death of Christ happened once on Calvary, and does not need to be repeated; it is sufficient for eternity.

If we say that Christ obtained redemption and then ladles it out to those who 'choose him', we are right back on the road to Rome. This, again, is precisely what the Catholic Church teaches. Earlier in this book we referred to the Catholic Church's concept of a 'pool of merit' that Christ and the saints obtained through their suffering. The sacraments are then the mode by which this excess merit is distributed. But this concept of grace is a reproach to the cross.

Contrary to the above teaching, the reformers taught that Christ's death actually purchased the redemption of those he came to save. That is, he died not to make *possible* the salvation of some, but *actually purchased* the salvation of the elect. The application of this redemption happens at the time of conversion according to the will of God. The death of Christ, therefore, was one hundred percent effective; all whom the Father gave to Christ were redeemed. To believe otherwise makes Christ a 'god' who tries his best, but often times fails.

Christ came to earth with the specific mission to save 'his people'. To hear those who believe in free will talk about it, you would think it was 'mission impossible'. This, praise God, was not the case. Jesus accomplished his mission in a glorious way. He now sits at the right hand of the Father enthroned in glory. He is not sitting on his throne biting his fingernails in hopes that somehow reprobate humanity will 'get it' and turn to the gospel. The fact of the matter is that men and women can never understand the gospel without the electing grace of God who shows mercy.

We need look no further than Colossians 1:13-14 to see that this is true. Here we are told we have been delivered from 'the domain of darkness' and transferred to 'the kingdom of His beloved Son ... in whom we have redemption, the forgiveness of sins.' This transfer is a one-dimensional affair in that God is the one doing the 'transferring'. Man and God were not pedalling in the same direction. Man was vigorously pedalling in the opposite direction. God chose some to be scooped up and rescued from pedalling off the cliff into the abyss.

We even see very clear intimations of this in the Old Testament. In Ezekiel God says that he is going to do a divine transplant operation on Israel. Since we are told in Gal. 6:16 that the church is the 'Israel of God', we can be assured that this applies to those who will come to faith in Christ. In Ezekiel 11:19, God tells us that he will give them 'one heart, and shall put a new spirit within them. And I shall take the heart of stone out of their flesh and give them a heart of flesh ...'

Yet again, it is God who is doing the action. The subjects in question have not had any kind of change of heart at present, and are in an idolatrous rebellion. It is God in his loving kindness that reaches down in the midst of all this and declares that things will change — and he will change them.

In Deuteronomy. 30:6, we also see the foreshadowing of Christ's redemptive work, for we are told '... the Lord your God will circumcise your heart and the heart of your descendants, to love the Lord your God with all your heart and with all your soul, in order that you may live'. The apostle Paul picks up this exact theme in Romans 2:29 when discussing who is a 'true Jew'. A true Jew is not one who is physically circumcised, but '... inwardly; and circumcision is that which is of the heart, by the Spirit ...' The key here is, 'by the Spirit', for it indicates that the regenerative process is one initiated, controlled and finished by God.

One of the amazing things about Christianity is that it took a symbol of total humiliation, the cross, and turned it into a symbol of total victory. The vicarious death of Christ on Calvary stands at the centre of all history. The work of Calvary is complete and eternal. The cross is *not* a symbol of 'positive thinking'. Christ did not face the cross in hopes of making something 'possible'; he actually accomplished the goal; the securing of redemption for his people. Christ is not the impotent god of the pagans who tires easily when his creatures misbehave.

Salvation is theoretical only to the pagan, not the Christian. Christians can say with assurance that God chose them in Christ from before the foundation of the world. They can know that the cross will never fail them; they are secure in the arms of their Saviour. Moreover, they can know that as they tell others about this glorious Saviour they will see the fruit of their labours, for those that were ordained to eternal life *will* believe.

The true effect of election on the believer should be humility. To think that God chose the Christian for some reason we cannot fathom to seat them high in the heavens is simply amazing. It should cause us to serve him with zeal and love him with every atom of our being.

11.
Double Jeopardy

In criminal law, there is something called the 'double jeopardy clause'. It states that once a person has been found innocent of the charges against him, he cannot be tried again for the same crime. In essence, the free will gospel 'violates' this law.

What the free will advocate says when presenting the gospel is that Christ died for you, and if you reject the gospel you will go to hell. You will go to hell because Christ paid the penalty for your sins, but you have rejected his sacrifice. Therefore, *you* must now pay the penalty for those sins. Even a secular lawyer would see the inherent contradiction in this scenario.

We can see this by taking a very simple example. A man commits a murder and is found guilty before a legitimate court of law. He is condemned to death by firing squad and is led outside to be shot. Suddenly a man steps out from the crowd and says, 'Don't shoot him. I will take the penalty of the court; shoot me!' The condemned man is then set free, and the 'substitute' is put in his place and shot dead. Still unsatisfied, the court reconvenes, tries the original suspect and decides, even though there was a substitute who paid the penalty, to kill him anyway. Once again, they grab him, tie him to a pole and he is shot dead.

Double Jeopardy

In the above example, was not the penalty paid by the substitute? Indeed, it was. Then why was the original suspect retried and shot? The answer is that there was a miscarriage of justice as the substitute took the penalty, but the original suspect was put into 'double jeopardy' by being tried again for the same crime — and then executed.

This same contradiction exists with the free will gospel. Christ dies for the sins of 'all' men and women and pays the penalty of God's wrath. Yet, if you reject that sacrifice, you can be tried and condemned for the *same* sins that Christ paid for. That is double jeopardy, and *that is not the gospel!*

From this we can see why Christ had to die for a *specific* people and not for everybody without exception. For if Christ paid the penalty for all men, then the power of sin would be broken in them and all would be saved. But the Bible in no way teaches universal salvation. It teaches, on the contrary, that Christ died for a specific people. All of the sins of these people have been paid for in full. They are now 'innocent' of the charges against them and must go free.

The model of unconditional election is the only one that makes sense when one ponders Christ's sacrifice. It says that Christ came to save 'his people' from their sins, and that this was accomplished at Calvary. All those he died for will come to faith in Christ, because their sins have been paid completely. When the Holy Spirit draws them, their hearts will willingly open to the truths of the gospel and they will be 'born again'. This is the glorious truth of the 'Good News' of Jesus Christ.

The free will model may appeal to the emotions and what we feel is 'just', but it is not based on the biblical data. It is a frightening thing to consider that the majority of evangelical pastors and evangelists may be preaching a gospel that has little to do with the one found in the pages of scripture. It is even a greater crime that there are many Christians who believe that God gave them a 'chance' and *they* took it. Unwittingly, they have committed themselves to a 'works based' salvation and are marching in lock step with Rome.

Of course, throughout church history there have been those who have tried to circumnavigate the issue by talking about the 'efficacy' of Christ's sacrifice. The argument is that Christ indeed died for all without exception, but that the application of that sacrifice is only for the elect. The scripture that is appealed to in this case is 1 Tim. 4:10:

For it is for this we labour and strive, because we have fixed our hope on the living God, who is the Saviour of all men, especially of believers. (NASB)

Now at first blush, this may seem to be a powerful verse in favour of the aforementioned position. It's power, however, evaporates like smoke when examined more closely.

How is it that God is 'the Saviour of all men'? Does this mean that Christ died for all men? There is nothing in the text that would support this conclusion. Even a cursory exegesis of this verse would not come close to yielding such a conclusion. So what does this verse mean? Consider this: each day men and women get up in the morning and go to work. They have food to eat and homes to live in. They watch their children grow up, go to college and get married, etc. The point is that God allows even the reprobate to have and do these things. In fact, we sometimes wonder, as scripture tells us, about the prosperity of the wicked. In this sense, God is the Saviour of all men in that that he gives even the reprobate good things. But he is especially the Saviour of believers because not only does he give them these things, but eternal life also.

As we have stated, man's natural inclination is to inject his will into the plans of God. Struggle as he might, the free will advocate cannot overcome the mountain of evidence that speaks to man's total inability, and God's sovereign election plan. If Christ died for someone, that individual cannot be 'tried' for the same sins that Christ made atonement for. He or she will come to Christ, and they will come willingly. Conversely, if Christ did not die for an individual, all of that person's intellectual resources cannot help them to believe; they will turn away from the gospel and thus be condemned.

You say that this is unfair? What is unfair is that men and women are all in rebellion against a holy God, but God reaches down to 'save some'. Fairness would mean God's wrath poured out immediately on all humanity without exception. Is this the kind of fairness the free will advocate would have us believe in? By the mercies of God, we hope that it is not.

12.
The 'Weeping Jesus' Syndrome

In an attempt to bring sinners to repentance, many pastors and evangelists will either start to weep, or begin to talk about the 'weeping Jesus'. This is the Jesus of the free will gospel, the one that is heart broken and frustrated because sinners will not repent after being shown so much love. After all, many a sinner has been told that Jesus is actually down on his knees begging them to be saved! Alas, many times his pleas go unheeded.

We do not mean to say that it is not legitimate for a preacher to *truly* weep for the souls of the lost. Most certainly there may not be enough sincere heart-felt compassion for those on the fast track to hell coming from pulpits across our world today. But there is a difference, however, between true emotion and the emotion that manipulates in order to bring about a 'free will' decision.

Nor are we saying that the image of Jesus weeping is foreign to the Bible, for it is not; Jesus wept at the tomb of Lazarus, and he also wept over Jerusalem. However, it is this second incident that gets most of the attention when the issue of free will is discussed. It would be most disingenuous and cowardly of this present work if we did not address this scripture and what it is teaching us.

The passage in question is found in Matthew 23:37-39.

Here we find Jesus lamenting — perhaps not actually weeping, for the text does not tell us this specifically — over Jerusalem's unbelief. Jerusalem is symbolic of the heart of the Jewish nation and cultus. It represents God's electing work and the earthly city of their locale. Jesus, however, calls this the city that '… kills the prophets and stones those who are sent to her!' (v.37). In a true sense, they have rejected the message of scripture and all the prophets who were trying to point them to Messiah, Jesus in particular. The second half of this verse is the ammunition that is used to 'prove' that by our own free will, we can decide for or against Christ: 'How often I wanted to gather your children together, the way a hen gathers a chick under her wings, and *you were unwilling*' [Emphasis added]. It is this 'unwilling' part that seems to engender all the attention.

When the Jews, for the most part, rejected Christ and his gospel, was it a free will decision based on well thought out circumstances? We must again insist that God has a plan, and that that plan cannot be thwarted. So then, why did the Jews reject Jesus?

The key to answering this question is found two chapters back in Matthew 21:33-34, the *Parable of the Wicked Tenants*. In this parable a wealthy landowner plants a vineyard. He puts a wall around it, digs a wine press, builds a tower and then rents the land out to sharecroppers. These are the 'wicked tenants'. He then goes on a journey. Obviously, a business arrangement has been made with these tenants that he would send his slaves into the field to gather his portion when harvest time came, which is precisely what he did. Successively, the tenants beat and kill the slaves that are sent by the landowner. Finally, the landowner sends his only son, for surely they will respect him. But he fared the worst and was immediately abused and killed

Our Lord then asks a question, 'When the owner of the vineyard comes, what will he do to those vine-growers?'

It is safe to say that these 'wicked tenants' are the Jewish leaders of Jesus' time. These are the ones that not only rejected Jesus and told others to do so, but also came from a lineage that rejected the holy prophets of old. What, therefore, do you think they are going to do with Jesus? Naturally, in this parable it is he who is the 'beloved son'.

The recipients of Jesus' parable give him the obvious answer to his question: 'He will bring those wretches to a wretched end, and will rent out the vineyard to other vine-growers, who will pay him the proceeds at the proper seasons'. (v.41)

Jesus then delivers the *coup de grace*:

'Did you never read in the scriptures,
'The stone which the builders rejected,
This became the chief corner stone ...' (v.42)

The leaders of the Jews, and vicariously the Jewish people, rejected Christ. The 'other wine-growers' are the Gentiles who would be more than willing to be a part of the Kingdom of God.

It was well within the plan of God to 'enlarge the tent' by bringing the gospel message to the Gentiles. If the Jews had accepted Christ and made him their Messiah, and most likely their earthly king, the 'gospel' would have been localized. But the coming of Christ marked the beginning of the end of 'Jewish particularism'. This all finally culminated with the destruction of the temple in 70 A.D. That is why the Paul tells us in 1 Thessalonians 2:15-16 that the Jews, '... both killed the Lord Jesus and the prophets, and drove us out. They are not pleasing to God, but hostile to all men ... hindering us from speaking to the Gentiles that they might be saved ... But wrath has come upon them *to the utmost*' [Emphasis added].

Honestly, you would be hard pressed to hear a sermon based on this passage from our 'politically correct' pulpits nowadays. This, however, is the Word of God, not the railings of a deranged anti-Semite.

Jesus himself made the mode by which the gospel would be initially spread clear; it would be received by a number of Jews at first, but then spread rapidly to the Gentiles. If we make a case for the Jews by their 'free will' rejecting the gospel, then we must assume that Christ went to 'plan B' in order for the message to be heard. This is patently absurd and is an affront to the sovereign will of God.

Must we believe, then, that God was absolutely in control of the rejection of the gospel by the Jews, but then asks all men to use their own wisdom to 'decide for Jesus'? This would make us to believe that God suffers from Multiple Personality

Syndrome; assuredly, he does not. Nor can we forge God into our own image with our own emotions and failings. This simply will never do.

We must believe in a God who pre-ordains all things, and then brings them to pass — to the letter. The forlorn, impotent god of the free will gospel is not the God of the Bible. Indeed, Jesus lamented over Jerusalem and its false teachers. Yet, even in this act he was carrying out the will of the Father for a greater purpose: not only would many Jews come to believe, but Gentiles also. God would call out *all* his people and make them of 'one blood'.

13.
Dealing With The Universal Texts

In 1 Corinthians 6:12, the apostle Paul declares that, for him, 'all things are lawful'. We also saw the interesting way the word 'all' is used in 1 Corinthians 15:22. We said earlier that context is of the utmost importance when examining God's Word. So when we look at Paul's statement, it would be ridiculous to take it at face value. *Everything* is lawful? Was murder lawful for Paul, or adultery, or stealing, or cheating? Of course not, and that is not what he is referring to. The context of Paul's declaration is Christian liberty juxtaposed to the Law.

So when we come across texts in the Bible that seem to teach that Christ died for all without exception, or that men and women have a 'free will' choice to 'choose Christ', we must examine them at close range in order to decipher what exactly is being said. Our stated goal at the beginning of this book was to make a case for the absolute election of the saints without stacking verses together. At this point, we will not be stacking verses for the other viewpoint, but we will be examining a few lest the reader claim we have not dealt with the issue fairly. Many reading these words may be ready to shout, 'but what about this verse … and this verse …'. etc. Obviously, there are many verses and many situations in the Bible that can be appealed to, but it is not within the scope of this present work to deal with them all. Yet, in the name of equal time, we will deal with some of the more obvious ones.

There are uses of language that, in their context, are idiosyncratic. We need look no further than the Gospels to see this in action. In Luke 2:1, we read that a decree went out from Caesar Augustus that 'all the world should be taxed' (KJV). Now, normally, we might be tempted to pass right over this verse, for really, what significance does it have for us today? The answer: Plenty, especially in the context of our discussion.

What is meant here by 'the world'? Does it mean that every man, woman and child were taxed? Some translations read, 'a census should be taken …'. In either case, was this phrase all-inclusive? Did the census cover every country in the world? Actually, this phrase refers specifically to the Roman Empire. Indeed, it was a great part of the world, but it certainly wasn't the whole world without exception. This is typical of the linguistic situations we find when dealing with the so-called 'universal texts'; what at first seems obvious is, upon closer examination, something quite different.

This same thinking can be applied to perhaps the most oft quoted text in the entire Bible: John 3:16. Here we are told that God 'so loved the world'. The free will believer usually makes a quantum leap in thinking when explaining this text. The reasoning goes that if the text says that God loved 'the world', this means He loved all without exception, and, as a further extension, wants to try to save everybody. Indeed, this kind of exegetical thinking has been used to the full by liberals and universalists, but does not find support upon closer examination. There are two Greek words that are used in scripture for 'world', *gay* and *cosmos*. The first word refers to the physical earth. The second refers to the inhabited earth, and this is the word that is being used in John's gospel. The word also implies a harmonious arrangement of something. In a sense, it means the aggregate of all things 'earthy'. Therefore, what is being referred to is the creation, including man, but *not* including all men without exception. Nowhere can we deduce from this text that Christ died for all inclusively.

But isn't it true that we read in 2 Peter 3:9 that God wishes 'all to come to repentance'? Now here is a verse that is misused even by many pastors and theologians who should know better, and is an example of not attending to the context. Peter is not making some kind of romantic, idealized statement regarding what God desires. If we go quickly to the very beginning of this chapter we see that he is writing to *believers*. Peter is writing to them because he is 'stirring up' their minds so that they can remember what the prophets and apostle said (vs. 1-2). In verse nine, we are told that the Lord 'is not slow about *His promise*'. What promise? The promise that he would come to save all of his people. Notice that the verse goes on to say that he is 'patient toward *you*'. The 'you' here are the believers that Peter is addressing, the elect. Thus, God is patient in that all the elect will come to repentance.

When looking at a theological point in the Bible, not only

should the particular verse be examined, but the entire chapter in which the verse is contained. The flow of the biblical writer's thinking must be fully taken into account, and that is what we have done here.

If we were hunting for another verse that is sorely misused, we would eventually find ourselves at Revelation 3:20. This is another case of a verse being used in an emotional and romantic way apart from sound biblical exegesis. 'Behold I stand at the door and knock;' Jesus says; 'if anyone hears My voice and opens the door, I will come in to him, and will dine with him, and he with Me.' Is this, as many free will believers claim, a clear call to all men to repent and believe; a universal call to salvation? Billy Graham once gave a sermon on this verse and said that Christ's knocking on the door of our hearts gets fainter and fainter as we grow older and our hearts get colder. Is this the thrust of this verse?

Again, we must examine the context of this verse in relation to its setting. Remember that chapters two and three of Revelation are taken up with the letters to the seven churches. These were actual churches in Asia Minor, modern day Turkey. Whether you believe as some that each church represents an epoch in church history, or whether you believe that the letters were only for each church at that specific time — or something in between — has no bearing on our particular analysis of 3:20.

In verse 3:14, we read: 'And to the angel of the church in Laodicea write: …' The message we read of in verse twenty is part of the entire pericope that speaks of Laodicea; it is a message to a particular church — and it is a message to *believers*. The Lord has something against this church; they are 'lukewarm'. The admonition is strong: they must repent of this or God will spew them from his mouth. Notice what it says in verse nineteen, a pivotal verse: 'Those whom I love, I reprove and discipline; be zealous therefore, and repent.' Again, this is clearly a message to believers, *not* the reprobate. They must amend their tepid ways. Therefore, verse twenty, this 'knocking on the door', is addressed to the heart of *believers*, not as some would say, the unbeliever. The believer is being called to a fervent life in Christ. This is not, as is obvious, a call to unbelievers to repent and believe the gospel. And yet we hear this very verse misused and thundered from many a pulpit.

Several chapters later in Revelation 7:9, we read of a great multitude 'which no one could count'. This is not, as some exegetes claim, the so-called 'tribulation saints' corresponding to Matthew 24. This multitude is rather the saved of all ages. What is important to our discussion, though, is how they are described. We are told that they come from 'every nation and all tribes and peoples and tongues ...'

The point here is that God, by absolute predestination, has called out for himself a people. This does not mean 'all people' in a universal sense. It means, properly, all *kinds* of people. It does *not* mean: 'All those people who made a decision for Christ.' Rather, these are the people that Christ came to save to fulfil the covenant within the Godhead. They are not the people for whom Christ made salvation 'possible'. They are the people for whom Christ actually purchased redemption. If this distinction is not clear, one can never understand the true teaching of the Bible regarding the mission of Christ and his redemptive work.

So what do we do when we go to the book of Hebrews and read that Christ tasted death 'for everyone'? (2:9). Does this mean that He died for everyone? We said that Adam's transgression resulted in spiritual and physical death for the human race. In order for Christ to identify with humanity, he had to take on human flesh. This is the doctrine of the Incarnation. Technically speaking, Christ was fully human, and yet fully divine. Theologians call this the *hypostatic union*.

When the Bible tells us that Christ 'tasted death for all', it is not saying that he 'died for all', but that he *identified* himself with all humanity. Jesus was called 'a man of sorrows' because he identified with frail, sinful, suffering humanity. Redemption, on the contrary, was a specific act whose purpose was decided in eternity past.

It is hoped that the reader is really grasping how important it is to understand the context of a particular verse as it relates to the overall themes of the Bible. An entire chain is useless if a link is removed. An engine will not function unless all the parts are properly installed. So too with the proper understanding of doctrine; the entirety of scripture must be considered before any conclusions are made.

The 'universal texts' present the believer in absolute predestination with some obstacles, but, as we have seen, by careful examination they are easily overcome. What we must do is look at the contents of the Bible from Genesis to Revelation as a continuum. Certainly, there are historical situations in the Bible that are set for a particular time and do not relate to us today. But it is the overall message that God is trying to convey to humanity that is vitally important to understand. It is the responsibility of the believer to ferret out the deeper meaning of the texts in question, rather than relying solely on the teachings of others. While God has given us pastors and teachers, he has not removed our responsibility to learn, know and walk with him in a more intimate fashion.

14.
The Benefits of Absolute Election

The fact that we have a Saviour who does not leave things to chance but assures us that he is totally in control should cause all anxiety to melt away. If we have truly trusted Christ as Saviour, we should know the benefits of being redeemed. As the great reformer Melancthon said: 'To know Christ is to know His benefits.' So we are obligated as believers to study the benefits of Christ, not to pad our egos in order to mock the unsaved, but rather to give glory to God for saving us from a Christless eternity.

Those who oppose the doctrine of absolute election fail to see the glory that it brings to the Creator. Contrary to being 'unfair', it is entirely fair because God, in His infinite wisdom, has made it such. He does not need to stand at the bar of human justice to explain his actions.

To put things in perspective, consider what humanity would have done had not God elected a people from before the foundation of the world. Would humanity willingly turn to the Saviour? Would they be able to reason out the meaning of the cross by themselves? The answer should be obvious; humanity would have nothing to do with the things of Christ, and no one would be saved.

The doctrine of absolute election speaks to the question of God's character. It says that he is all knowing and all loving.

It presents God as the one who truly knows what is best for the individual and the world at large. It wipes away man's arrogance and pride, and it replaces it with humble thankfulness. It tells the believer that they need not worry if they stumble along the path for they are 'sealed until the day of redemption' (Eph.4:30). Yet there are those who would go so far as to say that they can 'unseal' themselves and thus be lost. These people must consider the commentary they are making on the very nature of God, and how woefully inadequate their study of God's Word is.

If we do not believe in a God who elects solely for his purposes, then logically we must believe in a universe where entropy rules and men cower at the thought of what will happen tomorrow. However, the essence of faith is to put one's trust in the decision-making abilities of God, not on the happenstance of a random universe.

It is not surprising that even the reprobate gain from the sovereignty of God. Does not God allow them houses and cars and fame? Does he not hold back his righteous wrath so as to effect the salvation of the elect, whilst allowing the unsaved to live in earthly peace? The brilliant Puritan John Owen once remarked that God must think little of material possessions for He gave so much of them to the unsaved! In contrast, to the saved he gives eternal life and abundant spiritual blessings. Which would you rather have?

We may say then that there is a specific, regenerating grace applied only to believers, and then there is what philosophers call an 'epiphenomenon', or by-product, of the action of grace. So the result of election really, in some way, benefits all humanity. This returns us, yet again, to the concept of 'fairness'. The free will believer must consider all of these things before crying foul. God is merciful, but he is merciful on his terms, not ours. Mercy and vengeance belong to the Lord, and we as his creatures must accept how he doles them out, and to whom.

The free will believer would argue that grace is given to every man and woman, the only difference being the degree. This is an inadequate explanation of God's actions, and fails to understand what happened at Calvary. There is an absolutely qualitative difference between the elect and reprobate of this world. Let us take an example of two people as our paradigm.

Johnny and Suzie are both at an evangelistic rally. Both of them hear the gospel presented in a clear and understandable way. Yet, Suzie is converted while Johnny is not. Now we must ask the question: why? Specifically, what does Suzie have, intellectually, spiritually and otherwise, that Johnny does not? Why is Suzie's heart open to the gospel while Johnny's heart is cold and distant to it? The free will believer would say something like, 'Well, Johnny's heart is hard. By his own free will, he has decided not to follow Christ. Suzie, on the other hand, has opened her heart to the truth of Christ's offer of salvation'. So, if we are to state this situation plainly, Johnny has simply brushed off the Creator of the universe, while Suzie has 'invited him into her heart'. Can this be? Can men and women freely reject God's will while others can 'invite' him to perform? You would certainly have a hard time convincing the apostle Paul of this!

No, man cannot 'invite' or turn God away and thus manipulate or frustrate his plans. Men and women will respond or not respond to the gospel according to the pre-ordained will of God. That will is fair, just and merciful, and we should bow the knee to it, rather than trying to put the proverbial 'square peg in the round hole' by using human barometers to figure out God.

15.
Sorting Out The Issues

An encapsulation of all the issues we have raised would lead to the question we have asked repeatedly: Who is the final authority as pertains to our salvation? The answer to this depends on one's view of the finished work of Calvary. Indeed, if we believe that Christ's work on Calvary is finished, we cannot them toss the ball to fallen men and women and ask then to 'do something'. When in his dying breath our Lord proclaimed, 'It is finished', what exactly was finished? Did he do all that he could do to reach out to unredeemed humanity, only to have that very same humanity, for the most part, thwart his will?

If we then proceed to say that Christ 'elected' those whom he knew would choose him, we arrive back at the same conclusion, for where is the sovereignty of God in this? Either we have the sovereign God of the Bible, or we have deified men and women who can deny the Creator, manipulate his will, and then determine by human standards what is 'fair'. Again and again we have seen that, not only is this not the case, but that God, from eternity past, chose who would and who would not be saved according to his pleasure, for his reasons and according to his own counsel.

The physical universe is here because God 'didst create all things, and by Thy will they existed, and were created'

(Rev. 4:11). The God of the Bible is a creative God. He is the great 'I AM'. As such, he does not *need* humanity to make his being whole. But he has graciously created us to be partakers in his glory through Jesus Christ. Therefore, because Christ has been 'exalted above the heavens' (Heb. 7:26), *we* are appositionally placed high in the heavenlies with him, spiritually speaking. Does this not cause our finite minds to grope for words adequate enough to praise such a God?

Man can never claim any spiritual territory for himself. The exaltation of man's thinking over God's is at best foolishness, and at worst, devilish. It hearkens right back to the lie in the Garden, where Satan set the tone for fallen human thinking (Gen. 3:5). Somehow, humankind is under the impression that the passage of time has somehow improved their ability to reason through spiritual questions. But there has been no change in man's nature; he is separated from God by sin, and can in no way apart from the exacting intervention of God, be saved.

True believers must lay down their worldly thinking processes at the feet of their Saviour. They need to be 'transformed by the renewing' of their minds so that they 'may prove what the will of God is, that which is good and acceptable and perfect' (Rom. 12:2).

Suggested Further Readings

John Owen, *The Death of Death in the Death of Christ*, Banner of Truth

Abraham Kuyper, *Lectures On Calvinism*, Eerdman's Publishing

James R. White, *The Potter's Freedom*, Calvary Press

Edwin H. Palmer, *The Five Points of Calvinism: A Study Guide*, Baker

David N. Steele/Curtis C. Thomas, *The Five Points of Calvinism*, Presbyterian and Reformed

A. N. Martin, *The Practical Implications of Calvinism*, Banner of Truth

Duane Spencer, *Tulip: The Five Points of Calvinism in the Light of Scripture*, Baker/Revell

Peter Jeffery, *Believers Need The Gospel*, Calvary Press